BE THE BANK!

THE #1 INVESTING STRATEGY

BE THE BANK!

How to Profit by Creating High-Yield Interest Income

Be the Bank! is your guide, your GPS,
and your road map all rolled into one proven system.

BY JIM SEXTON

ISBN: 1508511241
ISBN 13: 9781508511243
Library of Congress Control Number: 2015902815
CreateSpace Independent Publishing Platform
North Charleston, South Carolina

DEDICATION

*To all of my family and loved ones who are still walking on earth…
and to those who have passed but are never forgotten.*

INSPIRATION

The real goodies in life are free.

The first of life's goodies is to have good health. It's true the first wealth is health.

The next set of goodies in life is family and friends. No matter how much money one has, it cannot compare to the wealth of family and friends.

I must also give thanks to live in a free country where people can write, travel, and own property and businesses as they choose.

INTRODUCTION TO

PRIVATE-MONEY LENDING

This book was written to pull back the curtain on how money, interest, and private lending come together to create one of the most fascinating and profitable businesses you can be in. Ultimately, what people and businesses want financially is cash flow. You will learn an entirely new business paradigm that creates cash flow using a high performing investment strategy backed by real estate.

This book does not show you how to start a bank, but you will be shown how you can act as a bank by lending money and collecting the interest, just like the banks.

The private-lending business has been around for hundreds of years, yet it is a business that very few understand.

This book will reveal to you a fact-proven, time-tested, income-producing financial system of lending money and collecting the interest.

You will learn how to make eye-popping yields of 10% to 30% on your money. Your world view of money, interest, and lending will be stretched, stimulated, and expanded in a way that will make you think you are in interest-rate heaven. If you are like most people, you're looking for a safe, reliable, high-yield income on your money. But it is difficult to solve the income problem when you don't have a road map to follow. *Be the Bank!* is your guide, your GPS, and your road map all rolled into one proven system.

In short, this book offers new ways of thinking and new ways of doing when it comes to investments.

CONTENTS

Chapter 1

THE FOUNDATION
OF *BE THE BANK!*

THE SECOND-OLDEST BUSINESS

This book is about sharing with you a business model that is hundreds of years old, yet it is one that very few people understand.

Lending money and collecting interest have been around forever. In the early years, say 300 BC and after, people who loaned money were called the moneylenders.

More recently, from the 1200s forward, the moneylenders took an image-marketing class and rebranded themselves. As part of the rebranding, they did away with the robes for suits and ties and renamed themselves the bankers.

As you will see, this book is a boots-on-the-ground insight into private lending. Wealthy individuals and average-income individuals can use the same strategies and financial principles that the banks use to make loans and collect the interest.

If you understand the banks' trade secrets, techniques, and methods and do what the banks do, you will earn the same high yields that the banks don't want you to know about. *Be the Bank!* will show you a systematic and detailed methodology to create 10% to 30% interest income.

Welcome to the world of private banking.

WHO HAS THE TALLEST BUILDINGS?

As the old saying goes, let's follow the money.

Go to the one hundred largest cities in the United States. Now, look up at the tallest, largest buildings in town.

What do you see? That's right—big signs on the buildings with names of banks and insurance companies.

Banks

The banks are direct on what they do. They loan money and collect the interest. The banks also offer other services that bring in fee income, but make no mistake—the banks' main business is loaning money and collecting the interest.

Insurance Companies

The words "insurance company" are another name for a bank. Yes, they have different operating systems, but the core business is the same...borrow at low rates, lend the money at higher rates, and collect the interest.

The insurance companies obtain their money by people paying insurance premiums; in bank terminology, insurance premiums are called deposits. The insurance companies then pay out claims; in bank terminology, claims are called withdrawals. Between the paid premiums and the claims paid, the insurance companies invest the money by making loans to individuals and other businesses and collecting the interest. The loans are made by subsidiaries of the insurance companies, so most of the time you don't realize the true lender is some large insurance company.

Big Business

Many people don't know that some of the biggest manufacturing companies make as much or more from financing their products as they do from making and selling the products. As an example, Ford and General Motors in some years have made more money financing their automobiles than they have manufacturing and selling the cars.

As you can see, the banks, the insurance companies, and the manufacturers all have one thing in common: lending money and collecting the interest.

In the end, the grand master of business is making loans and collecting the interest!

THE FINANCIAL SECRET OF MONEY

Be the Bank! wants to zoom out and take a thirty-thousand-foot view of money and interest. When we look at money and interest from thirty thousand feet, we can clearly see the financial secret of money. The following phrases are all we see at thirty thousand feet:

Those who *don't* understand interest pay it.

Those who *do* understand interest receive it!

If this book could be summarized, then the above quote is appropriate. That quote is the key to financial wealth.

Keep reading the above quote until the concept of collecting interest is marinated into your brain. Everything financial that you do must be seen through the lens of "Am I paying interest, or am I collecting interest?" You must reframe your thinking to grasp the magnitude of collecting interest.

THE INTEREST CLOCK

Unfortunately, with most businesses it may take one to three years before they start making a profit. In fact, some businesses never make a profit and go out of business.

Not so with *Be the Bank!* When you start your own private bank and make your first loan, you start earning interest (profit) the very next day.

When you loan money, the interest clock starts ticking now and continues to tick every twenty-four hours. The interest clock ticks every day, including all holidays.

Interest works even when you don't. Once you make the loan, you can be doing other things or vacationing anywhere, and your interest clock income stream is working for you 24-7!

Making loans and collecting interest can be done part time, or it can be a full-time business. Either way, the road map to wealth is owning an interest clock.

THE MAGIC OF COMPOUND INTEREST

The most amazing application of mathematical numbers is compound interest.

To tap into the money-making magic of compound interest, it's crucial to first understand how it works. Financially speaking, compounding is interest you earn on your principle and interest.

The interest or yield you can earn using the private-lending programs described in this book will produce outrageous returns of 10% to 30%.

In our examples below and the next two pages, we are going to use three different rates of return—10%, 14%, and 18%—to show you the monthly and yearly amounts of interest earned on interest-only loans and the compounding of those amounts.

Welcome to the world of money, interest, and magic!

Monthly/Yearly Earnings at 10% Interest-Only Loans	
$10,000	$83.33 mo. / $1,000 yr.
$100,000	$833.33 mo. / $10,000 yr.
$1,000,000	$8,333.33 mo. / $100,000 yr.
$10,000,000	$83,333.33 mo. / $1,000,000 yr.

Monthly/Yearly Earnings at 14% Interest-Only Loans	
$10,000	$116.67 mo. / $1,400 yr.
$100,000	$1,166.67 mo. / $14,000 yr.
$1,000,000	$11,666.67 mo. / $140,000 yr.
$10,000,000	$116,666.67 mo. / $1,400,000 yr.

Monthly/Yearly Earnings at 18% Interest-Only Loans

$10,000	$150 mo. / $1,800 yr.
$100,000	$1,500 mo. / $18,000 yr.
$1,000,000	$15,000 mo. / $180,000 yr.
$10,000,000	$150,000 mo. / $1,800,000 yr.

Annual Compound Interest: $100,000 at 10%

Year	Amount	Year-End
1	$100,000.00	$110,000.00
2	$110,000.00	$121,000.00
3	$121,000.00	$133,100.00
4	$133,100.00	$146,410.00
5	$146,410.00	$161,051.00
10	$235,794.77	$259,374.25
20	$611,590.91	$672,750.01
30	$1,586,309.32	$1,744,940.25
40	$4,525,925.62	$4,978,518.11
50	$11,739,085.45	$12,912,944.00

Annual Compound Interest: $100,000 at 14%

Year	Amount	Year-End
1	$100,000.00	$114,000.00
2	$114,000.00	$129,960.00
3	$129,960.00	$148,154.40
4	$148,154.40	$168,896.02
5	$168,896.02	$192,541.46

10	$325,194.85	$370,722.13
20	$1,205,569.29	$1,374,348.99
30	$4,469,312.15	$5,095,015.86
40	$16,568,729.30	$18,888,351.40
50	$61,423,946.40	<u>$70,023,298.90</u>

Annual Compound Interest: $100,000 at 18%		
Year	Amount	Year-End
1	$100,000.00	$118,000.00
2	$118,000.00	$139,240.00
3	$139,240.00	$164,303.20
4	$164,303.20	$193,877.78
5	$193,877.78	$228,775.78
10	$443,545.39	$523,383.56
20	$2,321,443.63	$2,739,303.49
30	$12,150,054.21	$14,337,063.97
40	$63,591,385.73	$75,037,835.16
50	$332,826,855.60	<u>$392,735,689.60</u>

Chapter 2

PULLING BACK THE
MONEY CURTAIN

WHY HAVEN'T I HEARD OF PRIVATE LENDING BEFORE?

Putting your money in the bank used to seem like a good idea until you saw the interest rate the bank paid you. Putting your money in the stock-and-bond market is the mantra of sales people making fees on your money.

Alternative Investments

Let's be clear—alternative investments do not equate with more risk than stocks, bonds, and real estate. *Be the Bank!* is about being in the lending business and collecting the interest. Loaning money and collecting interest is a time-tested, incoming-producing alternative that can provide you with a solution to the financial challenges of how to have money make money.

Unfortunately, you will not hear about loaning money and collecting the interest from your stockbroker, your financial advisor, your realtor, your insurance agent, or your banker. You see, none of these professions make any money, fees, or commissions when you act as your own bank and start loaning money and collecting the interest.

Your stockbroker wants you to buy stocks and bonds, so he or she can make a commission or fee on each transaction.

Your financial advisor wants you to buy stocks, bonds, or insurance products, so he or she can make a commission or fee on each transaction.

Your realtor wants you to buy real estate, so he or she can make a commission on the deal.

Your insurance agent wants you to invest in insurance annuities, so he or she can make a commission, and the insurance company can loan out your money and collect interest on it.

Your banker wants you to deposit the money in the bank, so the bank can loan out your money, keep the biggest part of the interest income, and pay you very, very little interest on your money.

It is worth saying again—the stockbrokers, the financial advisors, the realtors, the insurance agents, and the bankers do not make a penny when you act as your own bank.

They will tell you alternative investments are risky. They will tell you anything to get you to invest with them. They will tell you this for two reasons:

1. They don't make any money when you act as your own bank by making loans and collecting the interest.
2. They don't understand the concept of *Be the Bank!*, or they would be making loans with their money and collecting the interest.

COMPARE INVESTMENT STRATEGIES

Which frightens you the most: losing money in the stock market or seeing the lowest interest rates in history? You can, with knowledge and action, magnify and multiply your current interest income using *Be the Bank!*'s time-tested financial strategies to grow your money safely and predictably. A lot of people use their fear of the unknown as an excuse to go with the so-called safe investments at ridiculously low rates of return. With *Be the Bank!*, you can safely earn 10% to 30% with your money.

Now let's compare mainstream, fee-driven, commission-based investments with the *Be the Bank!* concept of making loans and collecting the interest.

How does the *Be the Bank!* strategy compare with other financial products? Let's compare the following:

- Stocks vs *Be the Bank!*
- Bonds vs *Be the Bank!*
- Real estate vs *Be the Bank!*
- Gold or silver vs *Be the Bank!*

<u>Stocks vs *Be the Bank!*</u>

In my opinion, investing in the stock market is a form of gambling. The people running the companies listed on the exchanges and the people working on Wall Street are always one step ahead of the average investor. With the stock market, you are always nail-biting to see which direction your money is moving.

Yes, there are companies on the stock market that produce dividends (another word for interest); however, these dividends don't compare to the 10% to 30% interest earned with *Be the Bank!*

The people running Wall Street and the companies on the stock exchanges are in the know and start selling their stock first when profits start going down because they have a front-row seat to the numbers before the public has access.

The Wall Streeters have information that the average investor will never have. In addition, the Wall Streeters, stockbrokers, and financial advisors want you to keep buying and selling stocks all the time. This is called "churning your money," because they make fees and commissions each time you buy or sell a stock.

It has been proven that some Wall Street companies were encouraging the public to buy a specific financial product while "shorting" the same financial product because they knew it was going to blow up financially. You can use any word you want, but where I come from, that's called fraud. The government slapped their wrists with a little fine, and the Wall Streeters continued to party in the Hamptons.

With the stock market, you just don't know. With *Be the Bank!*, you are in control of your investments.

Bonds vs *Be the Bank!*

Here is a fact that you won't hear from your stockbroker or investment advisor: bonds are actually loans cut up into little pieces and sold to investors.

That's right—bonds are loans. The bondholder earns interest just like a bank loan earns interest.

Even though all bonds are loans, there are different types of bonds: treasury bonds (loans to the federal government), state bonds (loans to individual states), municipal bonds (loans to cities and counties), and corporate bonds (loans to large companies). All of these bonds (loans) are sliced and diced into little portions that allow the average investor to participate in the loan and collect interest (very little interest).

Now that we know bonds are really loans, how do they compare with *Be the Bank!*?

When the big Wall Street firms originate the bonds (loans) for the borrowers, they take much of the income/fees that keep the bondholder earning less than they otherwise would.

In 2015, the ten-year treasury bond—which is a benchmark pricing for other bonds, mortgage rates, and investments—is floating between 2% and 2.2%.

As I will show you in a later chapter, you can safely and securely earn 10% to 30% interest income by being the bank, making the loans, collecting the interest directly, and cutting out Wall Street.

If you compare bonds earning 2.2% versus *Be the Bank!* earnings of 10% to 30% for ten years, the difference in interest earned is huge—see the section on compounding interest in the previous chapter. The hands-down winner is *Be the Bank!*

Real Estate vs *Be the Bank!*

Unlike the other investments that we are comparing to *Be the Bank!*, we like real-estate investments. The problems with real-estate investments are the three Ts of being a landlord:

- T = Tenants (Tenants can be exhausting.)
- T = Toilets (Repairs and remodeling are expensive.)
- T = Trash (Vacancies are dirty and costly.)

When you figure the actual dollar cost of real-estate ownership, it really lowers your rate of return or profit/income. Let's look at some of the costs of investing in real-estate ownership:

1. Repairs—It seems repairs are ongoing in rental units.
2. Remodeling—It can cost you thousands just to maintain the value of the property.
3. Property Taxes—They are always a lien on your property if not paid.
4. Hazard Insurance—You better pay for fire and liability insurance to cover your investment.
5. Vacancies—This money is lost forever, period.
6. Mowing, Landscaping, and Bug Exterminating—There are always miscellaneous expenses involved in owning investment property.
7. Management—This is another expense if you don't want to deal with the tenants, repairs, and vacancies.

Now let's look at the same costs when investing in a loan and collecting the interest:

1. Repairs—Zero cost (Owner is responsible.)
2. Remodeling—Zero cost (Owner is responsible.)

3. Property Taxes—Zero cost (Owner is responsible.)
4. Hazard Insurance—Zero cost (Owner is responsible.)
5. Vacancies—Zero cost (Never a vacancy; any money owed is added to the loan balance.)
6. Mowing, Landscaping, and Bug Exterminating—Zero cost (Owner is responsible.)
7. Management—Zero cost (Monthly interest check is sent to our PO box—easy.)

OK, I know, even with the negatives, real-estate investing can be a great investment because of leverage and potential inflation of property values; plus the tenant pays down the mortgage on the property.

So, here is my take on investing in real estate and loans made with *Be the Bank!* strategy:

- Buy some real estate to hold for long periods; and
- Buy some real estate to fix and flip, put the money in *Be the Bank!* loans, and make a regular interest-income stream without all the negatives of owning investment property.

Yes, you can be a landlord and a lien lord.

Gold or Silver vs *Be the Bank!*
Putting your money into gold and silver is not an investment—it's speculation.

Gold and silver do not create or produce any interest or income. Putting your money in gold and silver is strictly a speculative position that is based on the fact that the price of gold and silver *must* go up in value to make any money.

In fact, gold and silver are poor investments because they do not produce any income while you are holding the gold and silver.

As I will show you in a later chapter, you can safely and securely earn 10% to 30% interest income by making loans and collecting the interest. Because loans produce interest income, gold and silver must go up in value each year at least 10% to compare to making loans.

If you hold the gold and silver for five years, then gold and silver must go up in value by at least 50% just to stay even with the basic interest earned by being the bank, making the loans, and collecting the interest.

MYTHS AND FACTS ABOUT *BE THE BANK!*

- Myth #1: It All Seems So Difficult
  There is nothing difficult about loaning money and collecting the interest. Investing in loans may seem difficult because it's a new concept to most people.
- Myth #2: The Math Is Hard
  All the formulas and math expertise that you need to figure interest/yield are built into a basic financial calculator. It only takes a few calculations to figure your profits.
- Myth #3: The Paperwork Is Cumbersome
  Not really. The paperwork for each of the three lending concepts that we present in the next chapter is easily produced and understood.
- Myth #4: It Takes a Lot of Cash
  Cash is nice, but there are other sources of funds that you can use to earn interest from or share in the interest.
- Myth #5: I Could Lose Money
  If the paperwork is done correctly and you keep the loan-to-value much lower than the value of the property, you will receive all your money back with interest.

- Myth #6: It's Difficult to Find Borrowers
It is not difficult to find borrowers. There are plenty of people who are in need of money and are willing to pay a higher interest rate to obtain the loan.
- Myth #7: I Will Lose My Money if the Borrower Claims Bankruptcy
Not true. You will have a recorded first lien on the property. You cannot be wiped out if the borrower claims bankruptcy. The courts will order the borrower to continue with his or her payments. If the borrower continues to miss payments, you can proceed with a foreclosure process to sell the property. In both cases of a bankruptcy or foreclosure process, have a real-estate attorney represent you. In almost all cases, your actual legal costs to hire an attorney are added to the balance of the loan.
- Fact #1: Safety
Investing in loans can be one of the safest low-risk investments available. It provides the investor with the unique ability to analyze profits and potential dangers before ever making the loan.
- Fact #2: Good Yield
The interest/yield on loaning money can be mind-blowing. When you combine points (a point is 1% of the loan amount charged to the borrower) and leverage, you can earn interest yields from 10% to 30%.
- Fact #3: Cash Flow
Not all investments offer cash flow. Making loans and collecting interest is a cash-flow machine. Your money produces interest every twenty-four hours, and the money is sent to your PO box every month.

- Fact #4: Easy Management
Managing the loans is easy, unlike managing real estate with the tenants, repairs, and other issues involved. With *Be the Bank!*, you just track what is owed and what is paid.

Chapter 3

THE PRIVATE-LENDING
BUSINESS

THE THREE TYPES OF
PRIVATE-LENDING PROGRAMS

If your business approach or investment strategy is not generating the interest rates or yields that you are seeking, then each of the three private-lending programs described below will take you outside of your current mind-set and methods and show you how to massively increase your yield.

Be the Bank! created the concept of the subdivided loan, or SDL. Each of these three programs incorporates this concept that dynamically impacts basic loans to produce loans with incredibly high-octane yields.

OK, let's get started by reviewing the three types of private-lending programs:

1. Direct Lending on Real Estate
    In this type of lending, you are making direct loans on real estate at no more than 65% loan-to-value and earning an interest yield rate of 10% to 30%.
2. Owner-Financed Real Estate
    In this type of lending, the property is owner-financed, and you are earning an interest yield rate of 10% to 30%.
3. Purchasing a Tax-Lien Certificate
    In this type of lending, you are investing in a real-estate tax lien from the government that is a real-estate tax lien against someone's property. You are earning an interest yield rate of 10% to 30%.

OK, are you ready for another paradigm shift or another banking secret that you won't ever hear from your stockbroker, your financial advisor, your realtor, your insurance agent, or even your banker? Here it is.

The banks invest their money in all three of these private-lending programs! Yes, in the real world, the banks employ a methodology to maximize their yields by investing in all three types of lending programs.

1. Direct Loans
   Yes, obviously the banks make direct loans and collect the interest. This is the bank's core business.
2. Owner-Financed Real Estate
   Yes, the banks buy existing loans from other banks and insurance companies and collect the interest. The banks also buy owner-financed loans at a discount and collect the interest. The banks buy these loans directly, or more often, the banks own a subsidiary company that purchases the loans and collects the interest! The banks also owner-finance property that they own. If a bank forecloses on a property and no one buys the property at the foreclosure sale, then the bank is the new owner of the property. The bank can then sell the property and make a loan to the purchaser, thereby, owner-financing the property. The banks do not want to own real estate; the banks want the interest from financing real estate.
3. Tax-Lien Certificates
   Yes, the banks pay their depositors very low interest rates and then invest the money in tax-lien certificates at much higher interest rates and collect the interest. The banks buy these tax liens directly, or more often, the banks own a subsidiary company that purchases these tax liens and collects the interest.

The reason you won't hear about these three types of private-lending programs from your stockbroker, your financial advisor, your realtor, your insurance agent, and even your banker is because they don't make any fees, commission, or interest if you set up your own private bank and invest directly in these three types of private-lending programs.

You don't need the above professionals to invest in these three types of private-lending programs to earn high-yield interest income. If you know what the banks do with their money and follow the road that is already paved with high-yield interest income, you, too, can *Be the Bank!*

PRIVATE-LENDING PROGRAM #1—DIRECT PRIVATE LENDING ON REAL ESTATE

Be the Bank! makes direct loans on specific types of real estate and collects the interest. Before we go any further, let me make a very clear distinction on what types of direct loans that *Be the Bank!* makes and doesn't make on real estate.

Distinction #1

Be the Bank! does not make subprime loans. In fact, the loans that *Be the Bank!* makes are exactly the opposite of subprime loans.

The toxic subprime loans that the banks and mortgage companies made in the 2001–2008 time period were made at 100% loan-to-value. That means the borrower had no money or equity in the property; therefore, the borrower had nothing to lose. To think that these banks and mortgage companies made loans to people at 100% of the value of the property is insane.

In addition to making 100% mortgage loans, the banks and mortgage companies allowed the borrowers to take out these loans without regard to the borrowers' financial ability to make the mortgage payments.

The banks and mortgage companies, in their quest to make points and fees on these subprime loans, were not only insane—they were crazy insane!

Be the Bank! only makes loans that protect the lender and the borrower.

The loans protect the lender in that the maximum loan amount is 65% of the value of the property. This gives the lender a 35% equity position that ensures the lender will receive all his or her money back with interest. Many times the borrower needs less than 65% of the value of the property, thereby creating even more of an equity cushion for the lender.

The loans also protect the borrower by limiting the amount he or she can borrow on the real estate, thereby assuring that the borrower has equity in the property and can always sell the property to pay off the loan and have equity or cash to go forward.

In addition, by confirming the borrower's ability to make the mortgage payments, it makes it a good loan for the borrower and the lender. We never want a borrower to lose real estate due to nonpayment.

Distinction #2

Be the Bank! does not make real-estate loans on owner-occupied residential real estate. This is the type of property that the owner lives in. These types of loans are highly regulated, and the lender must be licensed to make owner-occupied residential loans. Because the owner lives in the property, the government has established many rules and regulations to protect homeowners from taking out a mortgage loan that may or may not be in the best interest of the borrower. Do not make any mortgage loans on owner-occupied residential property.

Be the Bank! makes direct mortgage loans on business real estate, such as investment property and commercial property. This is the type of real estate that the owner does not live in. These loans are business-to-business loans. The property may be empty or rented, or the owner may use the property for business purposes; however, the owner does not live in the property.

Because these loans are business-to-business loans, there are very few rules and regulations when making the loan. There is no company license or individual license required to make business loans at this time.

Now for the fun part! Let's follow the money. When you make a direct loan, the five items below are your determining factors:

1. The loan amount
2. The interest rate
3. The points (a point is 1% of the loan amount)
4. The length of the loan
5. The payment amount

The Interest Rate

You have two choices to make on the loan other than the actual interest rate you are charging.

Choice #1—Amortized Loan: The loan is amortized to pay down or pay off the loan over a specific period of time. Each monthly payment has a principal portion and an interest portion.

Choice #2—Interest-Only Loan: The loan is interest only, and no amount of the monthly payment is applied to the principal of the loan. On loans of five years or less, we prefer the interest-only option. It's like having a CD (certificate of deposit) in the bank, except you are the bank earning high-yield interest income!

As a private bank making business loans, you can charge the amount of interest and determine other terms of the loan that you and the borrower agree to. The most common range of interest rates for private lending is 8% to 15%.

Points
When making direct loans, always charge points on the loan to increase your yield/profit on the loan. The most common range of points charged for private lending is two to five points.

Length of the Loan
Some private lenders only make the term of the loan for six months to one year. Other private lenders make the loans up to three years. We prefer the two-year to three-year term because our goal is to have the monthly interest-income checks rolling in on a continuous two- to three-year period. It's like this: If you are making a high-yield, interest-income stream every month, why limit the fun to six months to a year when the interest "party" can last two or three years?

Now let's look at an example loan:

Property value:	$100,000
Loan amount:	$60,000 (60% loan-to-value)
Interest rate:	12% (interest only)
Monthly payments:	$600 ($7,200 yearly interest)
Points charged:	3 points (3 points = $1,800)
Term of the loan:	3 years (36 months)

The yield for the first year on the $60,000 loan is 15%. We collected $7,200 in interest income, plus $1,800 in points, for a total of $9,000 income, which calculates to 15% of $60,000.

The second and third years of the loan, we collected $7,200 interest income each year, which calculates to a 12% yield.

Another way to figure the numbers is to add up all three years of interest and the points to create a three-year average yield of 13% per year on the $60,000 investment.

Now let's look at another example loan:

Property value:	$100,000
Loan amount:	$60,000 (60% loan-to-value)
Interest rate:	13.5% (interest only)
Monthly payments:	$675 ($8,100 yearly interest)
Points charged:	5 points (5 points = $3,000)
Term of the loan:	2 years (24 months)

The yield for the first year on the $60,000 loan is 18.5%. We collected $8,100 in interest income, plus $3,000 in points, for a total of $11,100 income, which calculates to 18.5% of $60,000.

The second year of the loan, we collected $8,100 interest income, which calculates to a 13.5% yield.

Another way to figure the numbers is to add up both years of interest and the points to create a two-year average yield of 16%.

"Supersize" the Yield!

We are going to "supersize" our yields by using leverage. Leverage is one of the great secrets to building wealth. Through the use of borrowed money, we can make more loans and increase the yield on the loans. To create leverage, it is necessary to use money from sources other than our personal money.

Most people don't know the difference between interest rate and yield. Generally speaking, interest rate is the rate that the borrower is charged and pays. Yield is the rate of return that the lender actually receives. They are not the same.

Before we go any further, let me assure you that the banks fully understand the difference between interest rate and yield. The banks' business model is not based on interest rate but on the yield they earn on the loans.

The SDL, the Subdivided Loan

Be the Bank! has perfected the use of borrowed money by creating a financial technique called the SDL, or subdivided loan. Borrowed money invested along with personal money will skyrocket your yield.

Let's look at an SDL to supersize the yield:

Property value:	$100,000
Loan amount:	$60,000 (60% loan-to-value)
Interest rate:	12% (interest only)
Monthly payments:	$600 ($7,200 yearly interest)
Points charged:	(no points charged)
Term of the loan:	One year (12 months)

Now we are going to divide the loan into two equal parts of $30,000. We are going to fund the one portion with our money and fund the other portion using borrowed money.

For this example, we are going to borrow the money at 6% from one of three sources: (1) a bank line of credit or equity line, (2) friends and family wanting to earn 6% on their money, or (3) business associates or people in general wanting to earn 6% on their money.

Follow the Money (Interest-Only Loan)
Example #1

The borrower pays	$600 mo. / $7,200 yr.
$60,000 x 12%	
We pay our investor	<u>$150 mo. / $1,800 yr.</u>
$30,000 x 6%	
We are left with:	$450 mo. / $5,400 yr.

Our money earned $450 a month or $5,400 in one year. Using our financial calculator, the yield on our $30,000 investment is 18%.

Example #2

In this example, it is the same loan as above, except we are going to charge the borrower two points, and the loan is for one year.

The borrower pays	$600 mo. / $7,200 yr.
$60,000 x 12%	
The borrowed money earns	$150 mo. / $1,800 yr.
$30,000 x 6%	
Our money earns:	$5,400 yr. Interest
	$1,200 Points
	$6,600 Total

Our money earned $6,600 income in one year on our $30,000 investment, which calculates to a 22% yield.

Example #3

OK, let's put some steroids in our yield by raising the interest rate.

Property value:	$100,000
Loan amount:	$60,000 (60% loan-to-value)
Interest rate:	13.5% (interest only)
Monthly payments:	$675 ($8,100 yearly interest)

The borrower pays $60,000 x 13.75%	$675 mo. / $8,100 yr.
The borrowed money earns $30,000 x 6%	$150 mo. / $1,800 yr.
Our money earns $30,000 x 21%	$525 mo. / $6,300 yr.
	$675 mo. / $8,100 yr.

The yield on our $30,000 investment is 21%.

Example #4

In this example, it is the same loan as above, except we are going to charge the borrower three points, and the loan is for one year.

The borrower pays $60,000 x13.75%	$675 mo. / $8,100 yr.
The borrowed money earns $30,000 x 6%	$150 mo. / $1,800 yr.
Our money earns:	$6,300 yr. Interest
	$1,800 Points
	$8,100 Total

Our money earned $8,100 income on our $30,000 investment, which calculates to a really "crush-it" yield of 27%.

Before we do the next calculations, it needs to be pointed out that the SDLs, subdivided loans, are not limited to dividing the loan in half. The subdivided loan can be divided 75% borrowed money and 25% your money or, the reverse, 25% borrowed money and 75% your money or any percentage combination. Also, the borrowed portion of the subdivided loan can come from more than one source. You might get half the borrowed money from a friend and the other half of the borrowed money from an investor. Because there are so many ways to subdivide a loan, *Be the Bank!* aptly named this concept SDL, or sub-divided loan.

In the next two examples, we are going to blow this yield thing to the moon by charging 15% interest.

<u>Example #5</u>

In this example we only have $20,000 of our money to invest, so we will be borrowing $20,000 from a friend at 5% interest, and we will be borrowing $20,000 from an investor at 6% interest.

Property value:	$100,000
Loan amount:	$60,000 (60% loan-to-value)
Interest rate:	15% (interest only)
Monthly payments:	$750 ($9,000 yearly interest)

The borrower pays $60,000 x 15%	$750 mo. / $9,000 yr.
My friend earns $20,000 x 5%	$83.33 mo. / $1,000 yr.
The investor earns $20,000 x 6%	$100 mo. / $1,200 yr.

| Our money earns | $566.67 mo. / |
| $20,000 x 34% | $6,800 yr. |

The yield on our $20,000 investment is a mind-blowing 34%.

<u>Example #6</u>

In this example, it is the same loan as above, except we are going to charge the borrower five points, and the loan is for one year.

The borrower pays	$750 mo. / $9,000 yr.
$60,000 x 15%	
My friend earns	$83.33 mo. /
$20,000 x 5%	$1,000 yr.
The investor earns	$100 mo. / $1,200 yr.
$20,000 x 6%	
Our money earns:	$6,800 yr. Interest
	$3,000 Points
	$9,800 Total

Our money earned $9,800 income on our $20,000 investment, which calculates to an eye-popping, money-maker, supersized, killer yield of 49%.

That 49% yield is not a misprint. Loans like this are done all day, every day. It's called banking. Can you say, *"Be the Bank!"*?

Even though the banks don't charge 15% interest, their yield is even greater than all the examples above. The banks are only paying one-quarter of 1% to borrow money from the Federal Reserve, and they are only paying depositors 1%. However, the banks are loaning the money at 5% and 6% interest rates, thereby loaning the money at five times and more than the cost of their money, versus the three times the cost of our borrowed money in the examples above.

The banks also increase their yields into the hundreds of percentages using Fractional Reserve Banking. This fractional reserve banking permits the banks to loan more money than the bank is holding in deposits on reserve, thereby creating more loans out of a digital bookkeeping entry. Only the banks are allowed to create money. Do not try this at home. This is one part of banking that you do not have the ability to mirror the banks' lending strategy due to laws that keep you from printing money.

PRIVATE-LENDING PROGRAM #2— OWNER-FINANCED REAL ESTATE

Owner-financed real estate creates high-yield interest income. There are two distinct types of programs for investing in owner-financed real estate.

Subtype #1—Buying Discounted Loans

There are many sellers of real estate who will owner-finance their property for multiple reasons. Some of the reasons might be because they can't sell the property because the price is too high, the property may need remodeling, or the buyers don't qualify for a traditional mortgage to buy the property.

When owners sell a property by owner-financing, they are acting as the bank by collecting payments over the term of the loan.

After the transaction closes, the seller of the property collects the monthly payments. If the loan is an interest-only loan, the payments will be all interest. If the loan is an amortized loan, then each monthly payment will have a principal portion and an interest portion.

As time passes by, the seller of the property, who has been collecting monthly payments, may decide that he or she would rather have *all* the money now instead of the monthly payments. Some of the reasons for wanting all the money now might be to help the children or grandchildren with college costs, to retire to Florida to escape the cold winter months, or even because of a business opportunity that requires a cash investment.

Now, this is where you come into the picture.

The seller of the property wants a lump-sum cash amount rather than to continue collecting the monthly payments. You can make an all-cash offer to purchase the owner-financed loan at a discount to face value and create a high-yield income stream!

What do I mean by "discount to face value"?

You will be buying the loan for less than the current balance on the loan. An example would be if the current balance on the loan is $80,000, you would purchase the loan from the seller of the property for $60,000 to $65,000.

Why would the person sell the loan for less than what is owed on the loan? Because, as stated earlier, he or she wants a lump sum of cash now rather than to collect payments over a longer period of time.

Once the loan is sold to you, the buyer of the property continues to make the same exact payment amount each month to you. Nothing changes for the buyer of the property except to whom and where to send the monthly payment.

Let's Follow the Money
The original terms of the loan when the property was sold are as follows:

Financed amount:	$90,000 (Amortized Loan)
Interest rate:	7%
Term of loan:	25 years
Monthly payments:	$636.10

After the seller of the property has been collecting payments for six years, the balance on the loan is $80,000. You make an offer to the seller, and the seller accepts a cash purchase price of $60,395 for the loan.

Your yield on the loan is 12%.

How did we come up with a 12% yield and a purchase price of $60,395? Using a financial calculator and knowing the terms of the original loan and the current balance, you can enter the numbers into a financial calculator and instruct the calculator to identify the exact purchase price of the loan to give you a 12% yield over the remaining term of the loan.

If you want to earn a 15% yield with your money on the same loan, you would enter the numbers into the calculator, and it would show you that you will need to purchase the loan for $49,663 to earn a yield of 15%.

Increase Your Yield!

We are going to increase our yield by using leverage. Leverage, or borrowed money, will increase the yield from medium size to extra large.

As explained in the previous section, we are going to apply the SDL, or subdivided loan, concept to maximize our yield.

Let's Follow the Money

This is the same original loan as described above:

Financed amount:	$90,000
Interest rate:	7%
Term of loan:	25 years
Monthly payments:	$636.10

The difference this time is that when we buy the loan for $60,395, we are going to purchase the loan with $30,197.50 of our money and $30,197.50 of borrowed money at 6% interest.

The borrower pays:	7% interest / $636.10 mo.
The borrowed money earns:	6% interest / $222.28 mo.
You receive the difference	$413.82 mo.
each month:	

You have $30,197.50 of your money invested, and you collect $413.82 each month for the remaining nineteen years of the original loan. Using your financial calculator, this gives you a 15.57% yield.

Subtype #2—Selling Property You Own

Selling property that you already own by owner-financing can create a high-yield interest income. There are two levels of owner-financing property that you can own. When you owner-finance property, you are acting as the bank by making a loan and collecting the interest.

Level #1

Level one is the owner-financing of property you already own.

Let's Follow the Money

Sales price:	$100,000
Down payment:	$10,000
Amount financed:	$90,000 Amortized

You and the buyer agree to a 7% interest rate for twenty-five years with monthly payments of $636.10. Earning 7% on your money is much better than what the banks are paying now.

Supersize Your Yield!

Again, we are going to use the SDL, or subdivided loan, concept to maximize our yield. We want to sell 50% of this loan to an investor who wants to make a comfortable 5.5% on his or her money. We are selling 50% of the loan for $45,000.

The borrower pays:	$636.10 mo.
The investor earns 5.5%:	$276.34 mo.
You receive the difference:	$359.76 mo.

You have $45,000 invested of your money, and you collect $359.76 each month. Using your financial calculator, this gives you an 8.42% yield.

Additionally, you now have the $45,000 cash to invest from the investor who bought 50% of the loan. You can put the $45,000 to work in a direct loan on real estate and make 12% to 30% interest. Combine the two loans, and you are earning a yield in the range of 12% to 16%.

OK, let's take this "yield thing" up a notch.

Level # 2—Buying Foreclosures

Buying foreclosures is like printing money. You can buy property at discount when buying foreclosures and then immediately sell the property at market value by owner-financing it.

Here Are the Numbers

We are going to buy a foreclosure at 20% below market value, and then we are going to owner-finance it using the SDL, or subdivided loan, concept.

Market value of the property: $100,000
Our purchase price of the property: $80,000
Purchase price to the new buyer: $100,000
Financed amount: $100,000 (amortized loan)
Interest rate: 8%
Term of loan: 15 years
Monthly payments: $955.65

We are going to sell 50% of the loan to an investor who wants to make a comfortable 5.5% on his or her money. In this example, we are selling 50% of the $100,000 loan amount, which is $50,000.

The borrower pays: $955.65 mo.
The investor earns 5.5% on his
or her $50,000: $408.54 mo.
You receive the difference: $547.11 mo.

Since you paid $80,000 for the property and received $50,000 from the investor, you now only have $30,000 invested in the loan. Using your financial calculator will show you a yield of 20.92% on your $30,000.

In addition, you have the $50,000 cash to invest in another high-yield loan at 18% to 30%, thereby creating high-octane interest income—just like the banks.

PRIVATE-LENDING PROGRAM #3—
PURCHASING TAX-LIEN CERTIFICATES

Be the Bank! earns high-yield interest income investing in tax-lien certificates, and the government guarantees the interest rate. So what is a tax-lien certificate?

All property owners pay property taxes on their real estate, except a few tax-exempt organizations such as churches and public buildings. The cities and counties depend on the collection of property taxes to fund and operate roads, schools, libraries, and other public services.

When a property owner does not pay property taxes, he or she is in default, and the taxing authority is short those funds to run and operate the public services.

The cities and counties must have a legal and forceful way to collect all property taxes to operate the public services. In the United States, each state has chosen between two different legal avenues to collect past-due property taxes. The two ways are tax-deed avenues and tax-certificate avenues.

Tax-Deed States

In tax-deed states, the taxing authority auctions off the property to the public to receive the money for past-due property taxes. The city or county files with the court system, and they can legally auction off the property to pay the past-due property taxes. The highest bidder receives a tax deed to the property. The property tax is a property lien over any mortgages, judgments, etc. In the next section is a list of tax-lien certificate states only. All the other states are either tax-deed states or states with a hybrid of tax-deed and tax-lien certificates. We prefer to keep it simple and only invest in the states offering tax-lien certificates only.

Tax-Certificate States

In tax-certificate states, the taxing authority auctions off to the public a tax lien, which is the amount of the past-due property taxes for each year on a specific property.

The investor bids on the interest rate he or she is willing to accept for paying the past-due property taxes on each specific property. In some tax-certificate states, such as in Florida, you can buy tax liens directly from the taxing authority at an 18% interest rate in addition to auctioning the tax certificates to the public.

The taxing authority receives the money from the investor to run and operate the public services without interruption. The taxing authority—the government—then gives the investor a piece of paper aptly named a tax-lien certificate. This tax-lien certificate is filed with the local taxing authority as proof that the owner of the property now owes the investor the past-due property taxes, plus *interest!*

Remember, past-due property taxes have a priority lien over all mortgages, judgments, and other liens on real estate. There is no better financial position to be in than owning a tax lien on real estate.

Each state that offers tax-lien certificates has its own set of rules and regulations on the interest rates offered and the bidding process. We suggest you focus on just one or two states and become an expert in those states. The interest rates in the tax-certificate states vary from 4% to 24%.

Now, here is a part you are going to love. You do not collect the back taxes from the property owner. The local taxing authority collects the back taxes and sends you your money with interest.

You do not need to live in a state that offers tax-lien certificates to bid in person or bid online to purchase the certificates. The public is welcome to bid wherever they live.

When I first started investing in tax-lien certificates, I checked the local taxing authority's public records and saw that some regional banks owned millions of dollars of tax-lien certificates. As mentioned earlier, the banks borrow money from depositors at 1% interest, and they invest in tax liens earning much higher interest rates. Can we all say, *"Be the Bank!"*?

There are many books available that give you all the details in purchasing tax-lien certificates. This book introduces you to the concept of tax-lien certificates and collecting the interest—just like the banks!

Here is a list of tax-lien–certificate states:

- Alabama
- Florida
- Iowa
- Wyoming
- Montana
- North Dakota
- South Dakota

- Arizona
- Illinois
- Kentucky
- Mississippi
- Nebraska
- Oklahoma
- Vermont

- Colorado
- Indiana
- Maryland
- Missouri
- New Jersey
- South Carolina
- West Virginia

Let's Follow the Money

When purchasing a tax-lien certificate, the property owner does not make monthly payments to you or the taxing authority. The property owner is required to pay all the property taxes owed to you, plus interest, at one time. You might have to wait two or three years to collect your money with interest, but that's fine. At 18% interest per year, we are in no hurry.

Because you can earn interest rates of 4% to 24% per year, you set the interest rate you are willing to accept in return for purchasing the tax-lien certificate. We have found an 18% interest rate works best for us.

Example:

Buy multiple tax liens: $60,000 x 18% = $10,800 yearly interest
If you get paid off in two years, you make $21,600.
Your yield is a whopping 18% per year.

Increase Your Yield!

We are going to increase our yield by using leverage. Leverage, or borrowed money, will increase the yield from medium size to supersize. As we did earlier, we are going to utilize the SDL, or subdivided loan, concept to maximize our yield.

This is the same purchase as above, buying multiple tax liens for a total of $60,000. This time we are going to borrow $30,000 from an investor at a 6% interest rate.

The property owners pay:	$60,000 x 18%	$10,800 yearly interest
The investor earns:	$30,000 x 6%	$1,800 yearly interest
You receive the difference:	$30,000 x 30%	$9,000 yearly interest

Using your financial calculator, you earned $9,000 a year on your $30,000 investment. That works out to a killer yield of 30%.

WHO BORROWS MONEY AT THESE HIGH RATES?

The borrower's only "rule" when borrowing money for three years or less is the following:

> IT'S NOT THE COST OF MONEY THAT COUNTS—
> IT'S THE AVAILABILITY!

That's right—there are many people and circumstances in which the cost of money is not the issue, but the availability of the money is everything. We are not talking about thirty-year loans at high interest rates. People will borrow money at high interest rates if it is for three years or less to solve a problem or to take advantage of an opportunity.

Making Direct Loans

There are many reasons why borrowers will pay a higher interest rate. The reasons are as varied as the circumstances. Some borrowers actually have good credit and can go to the banks and borrow at much lower interest rates. However, they don't want to wait forty-five to sixty days to find out if the bank said yes to the loan. The borrower may have a business opportunity that requires him or her to close on the deal in a very short period of time.

Then there is the group of borrowers who has investment or commercial property and may need to borrow money for remodeling, paying back-property taxes, or even buying out a partner. Again, the reasons are as varied as the circumstances are. Solving a problem is more important than the cost of the money!

Owner-Financed Real Estate

Buyers of real estate are willing to pay higher interest rates when an owner is willing to sell them the house and owner-finance it. The borrower may not qualify for a traditional loan and is happy to have the seller finance the property for them. Some people have a good income but don't have much for a down payment, so buying owner-financed real estate makes sense. Some borrowers just don't want to deal with the banks and all the regulations and paperwork required to obtain the bank loan. Again, the reasons are as varied as the circumstances are.

Tax-Lien Certificates

Property owners don't pay their property taxes for one of two reasons. First, they don't currently have the money. Secondly, their money may be tied up, and they can't get to it. Regardless of either reason, they must pay the interest rate that the investor bought the tax-lien certificate at.

Basic Guidelines on Making Loans, Purchasing Loans, and Purchasing Tax Liens

1. Never, never, never make an unsecured loan.
2. Always confirm that what you are loaning on is at least 30% more valuable than the loan amount.
3. Never make loans on things that depreciate or are moveable. Don't loan on cars, boats, and furniture that depreciate in value and are moveable. Don't loan on jewelry, art, and collectibles that are easily moveable and can be unidentifiable as the collateral.
4. Only make loans on real estate. There is a reason the word "real" is in real estate.
5. Never make a loan that you later regret and say, "If I had known that, I would not have made the loan." Do your due diligence!

Chapter 4

YOUR PRIVATE BANK

SETTING UP YOUR PRIVATE BANK

Setting up your private bank is an easy process. First, you must come up with a name for your private bank. Second, you will need to create a legal entity called a limited liability company (LLC). You can have your attorney draw up the papers. Many states have online forms in which you fill in the blanks and then pay a fee, and you just created your limited liability company or your private bank.

Next, open a checking account under the name of your limited liability company and fund the account with some money. From this point forward, all loans are funded out of this account, and all interest payments and payoffs are to be deposited into this account.

Purchase business cards with the name of your company and your contact information. Procure a PO box to have all payments and correspondence sent to. It all works best if you have a computer and a copier/fax/scanner to help you run your bank. Put all pertinent loan information, notes, and files in a locked filing cabinet for safekeeping.

Set up your systems to make loans, purchase loans, and track loans. Your bank is to operate with low, low overhead. Do not go out and rent office space until you are making big bucks and you need space and staff to help you collect and count the money.

Now get ready to start collecting interest!

A DAY IN THE LIFE OF A MONEYLENDER

Now that your private bank is set up to collect interest, let's take a look at a moneylender's day.

Thirty days a month...

Moneylenders don't have a "real job" in the sense that they can come and go anytime, anywhere. How can they do this? Well, they can do this because checks keep showing up at their PO boxes.

Seven days a week...

Just as you sharpen a saw to cut down a tree, you need to sharpen your business skills to run your bank. As a private bank, you need to sharpen your business by being organized, being detailed, and having systems in place. You should always be adjusting your systems and trying to simplify them while making improvements.

A day in the life...

There are four basic jobs of a moneylender:

1. Finding the money to invest
2. Finding the deals to invest in
3. Closing the transactions
4. Tracking and collecting

Finding the Money to Invest

Finding the money to loan is the lifeblood of your bank. There are three primary sources of funds:

Source #1—Use your own money.

Source one consists of our cash, savings, stocks, bonds, gold, and real estate, which can be sold or refinanced.

Source #2—Banks have plenty of money.

Source two consists of borrowing money from the banks, such as an equity line or line of credit, at low interest rates and loaning the money out at high interest rates. The bank will need collateral such as the notes created by the loans you make, real estate that you own, and other assets.

Source #3—People hate the low rates that the banks pay.

Source three consists of third-party investors such as friends, family, business people, or anybody who wants to earn more interest than they can at the bank. You can make a spread by paying the investors a decent interest rate and collecting a much higher interest rate—just like the banks! Just be sure to talk to your attorney before borrowing money from the general public.

Finding the Deals to Invest In

First, once it is known that you are a private lender, you will get referrals from other people, and you will get repeat business.

Here is a list of things that we do to attract loans: We have a website, we pass out business cards, and we pass out flyers to let people know what we do. We let the realtors know. We let the bankers know. And we let the attorneys know. We go to auctions. We go to investor meetings. In fact, we let everybody know what we do.

Closing the Transactions

Whether it be making a direct loan, purchasing an existing loan, or purchasing a tax lien, you must learn and be familiar with all the paperwork and legalities involved in closing the transactions. Using an attorney versed in these types of transactions is highly recommended. Once the loan or purchase is closed, keep the paperwork in a filing cabinet under lock and key. The note or certificate securing your money needs to be in a secure place.

Tracking and Collecting

Once the loan or purchase closes, it's time to start collecting the interest. It all starts at the post office. Having all payments sent to your PO box keeps it simple. Once you receive a payment, you need to use a spreadsheet, collections software, or another way to track payments as paid, due, balance, etc.

There are times when a borrower insists on not making payments. That's when you send a certified letter to them requesting payment. If you made the correct analysis when you made the loan, there is plenty of equity in the property. If the borrower still insists on not paying, turn the file over to an attorney familiar with these types of transactions. Either way, with equity in the property, you will get all of your money back with interest.

THE BUSINESS-VACATION PLAN

The business-vacation plan is simply doing business in areas of the country that you like to vacation in. That's right. The goal is to *Be the Bank!* not only in your home state and city area but in areas you like to travel to and vacation in.

The first step is to identify one or two areas of the country you like to vacation in. It might be the coast of the Carolinas, the Florida Gulf Coast, the deserts of Arizona, or the mountains of Colorado.

The second step is to identify the opportunities in these vacation areas that your private bank can use to create interest income to pay for your vacations.

The third step is to implement your system in these destination areas where you spend the *minimum* time doing business and the *maximum* time enjoying golfing, skiing, boating, hiking, walking on the beach, watching the sunsets, and eating at fabulous restaurants.

Road trip...

Just wanting or thinking about being the bank doesn't make it happen. We need a road map or a GPS to follow and guide us. OK, here we go. Put on your seat belt and buckle up for a little ride to success.

The first part of our journey is to recognize that it is our responsibility to make *Be the Bank!* a reality. It's the person in the mirror who is totally responsible to make that happen.

The second part of our journey is that you must have a clear-cut goal or objective. The goal or objective can be created by using vision and imagination. By using your mind through vision and imagination, you can set your goal picture. The goal picture is the way you want your life and your business to look.

The third part of our journey is to implement specific actions.

1. Obtain the right knowledge. Know what you are doing.
2. Identify the problems or roadblocks between you and your goal.
3. Use resources like counselors, advisors, and experts in resolving problems.
4. Create continuous action toward your goals and vision.

Destination…just ahead.

Once you have created your private bank in the state or area you live in, you can then reproduce your system in an area you like to vacation in and have your bank pay for your vacations. To sum it up, this really is having your cake and eating it, too!

BANK-TO-BANK

This book was written to share with you the concept of making or purchasing loans and collecting the interest—just like the banks.

This book was not written or intended to get into the weeds by explaining every little detail or providing dozens of pages of forms and example paperwork for each of the fifty states.

There are many books, magazines, articles, seminars, organizations, mentors, counselors, business people, mortgage lenders, investors, and attorneys who can guide you through the step-by-step process for each of the three private-lending programs in this book.

I know that each of the three private-lending programs works because this is what we do. I know that the high yields are real because this is what we do.

You have a choice...You can be the bank's customer—or you can *Be the Bank!*

If your private bank would like to talk to our private bank, contact us at the following:

Jim Sexton
540-777-7070
bethebank777@yahoo.com

All I dream of is
collecting interest.
It's good to
Be the Bank!